THIS BOOK BELONGS TO:

_____

PELICAN PUBLISHING
New Orleans

123s of NEW ORLEANS

WRITTEN + ILLUSTRATED BY:
NICHÓL BRINKMAN

The word "Pelican" and the depiction of a pelican are
trademarks of Arcadia Publishing Company Inc. and are
registered in the U.S. Patent and Trademark Office.

ISBN 9781455627288
Ebook ISBN 9781455627295

Printed in Korea

Published by Pelican Publishing
New Orleans, LA
www.pelicanpub.com

1

【 KING CAKE 】

KNIFE IN THE BOX

2

SWANS IN THE LAKE

3

MARDI GRAS FLOATS

4

JAZZ MUSICIANS

SHOTGUN SINGLES

SNOBALLS BEING SLURPED

FLEUR LADIES

KIDS ON THE LADYBUG

CEMETERY SPIRITS

DOGS IN THE KREWE

FERNS ON THE GALLERIES

MARDI GRAS THROWS

CRAWFISH IN KREWES

PEOPLE FESTING

GLOSSARY

KNIFE IN THE BOX

King cake is eaten during Mardi Gras season. It has a tiny baby hidden inside of it. Make sure to always leave the knife in the box for the next person that wants a slice!

SWANS IN THE LAKE

Big Lake at City Park is home to both real swans and paddle boat swans.

MARDI GRAS FLOATS

No Mardi Gras parades are complete without beautiful and elaborate floats!

JAZZ MUSICIANS

New Orleans is the birthplace of jazz music. You can hear it all over the city!

LAISSEZ BOYS

The Laissez Boys roll in Mardi Gras parades on personalized La-Z-Boy recliners that sit atop motorized scooters.

SHOTGUN SINGLES

Shotgun homes are long, rectangular, narrow homes. In New Orleans they are painted every color of the rainbow!

SNOBALLS BEING SLURPED

Beat the summer heat of New Orleans with a snoball: flavored syrup poured over shaved ice. Pick your flavor from Tiger's Blood to Wedding Cake!

FLEUR LADIES

The Krewe des Fleurs are a beautiful Krewe of ladies dressed like flowers that they construct themselves!

KIDS ON THE LADYBUG

The Ladybug is everyone's favorite roller coaster at Carousel Gardens: a carnival under City Park oak trees!

CEMETERY SPIRITS

New Orleans is one of the most haunted cities in America. Stop by a mysterious cemetery in the city and try to spy a ghost!

DOGS IN THE KREWE

A local favorite: the Mystic Krewe of Barkus is a parade full of dressed-up dogs. What is cuter than dressed-up dogs on parade?

FERNS ON THE GALLERIES

New Orleans has just the right climate for flora and fauna to flourish. Large ferns hang from many balconies in the city.

MARDI GRAS THROWS

Mardi Gras throws are tossed to parade goers from floats. One can catch anything from necklaces and doubloons to Moon Pies and rubber chickens!

CRAWFISH IN KREWES

Some of the krewes represented by these crawfish are: the Leijorettes, the Rolling Elvi, Chewbacchus, Rex, Luchador Krewe, Skeleton Krewe, and the Stompers. Can you name any more that you see?

PEOPLE FESTING

Jazz Fest is a 10 day music, food, art and culture festival. It is a celebration of life and living. Put on your crazy patterned button-up and dance in the grass!

DRAW CRAWFISH GIRL!

DRAWING IS FUN!

ABOUT THE AUTHOR-ILLUSTRATOR

NICHÓL BRINKMAN IS A LOUISIANA-BASED ARTIST. SHE DRAWS, PAINTS, MAKES CHILDREN'S BOOKS, AND SEWS SOFT SCULPTURES OF CHARACTERS SHE DESIGNS. HER FAVORITE FLAVOR SNOBALL IS WEDDING CAKE. SEE MORE OF NICHÓL'S ART ON HER SITE: WWW.PINKCHEEKSSTUDIOS.COM.